Renate Sueltz & Uwe H. Sueltz

Dr. Jutta Sueltz

My

BLOOD PRESSURE DIARY and PULSE LOG BOOK

BoD - Books on Demand

Norderstedt 2019

Bibliografische Information durch die Deutsche Nationalbibliothek

Die Deutsche Nationalbibliothek verzeichnet diese Publikation in der Deutschen Nationalbibliografie; detaillierte bibliografische Daten sind im Internet über http://dnb.dnb.de abrufbar.

Herstellung und Verlag:

BoD – Books on Demand, Norderstedt

ISBN 9-78374-9-43311-7

Through our arteries blood flows under pressure, this is called blood pressure. The blood pressure is highest when the heart contracts and the blood is forced into the vessels (systole).

Thereafter, the heart muscle relaxes and the blood pressure reaches its minimum value (diastole).

Too high, permanent blood pressure is called hypertension, hypertension. If it is too low, it is called hypotension.

The optimal values are at the upper value (systolic pressure) up to 120 mmHg and at the lower value (diastolic pressure) up to 80 mmHg. Hypertension begins at 140/90 mmHg.

Help your doctor to quickly detect high blood pressure or low blood pressure. He may also advise you to check and write down the blood pressure at home. Your doctor will tell you exact times. Otherwise, you start in the morning after getting up. After lunch and again in the evening. Before the measurement you should rest and be relaxed. Think of something beautiful. The wrist-measuring device is necessarily kept at heart level. Perform the measurements regularly.

Your health will thank you!

BLOOD PRESSURE AND PULSE LOG

MY NAME

MY DOCTOR

IMPORTANT INFORMATION

DATE TIME	BLOOD PRESSURE	PULSE	NOTES

DATE TIME	BLOOD PRESSURE	PULSE	NOTES

DATE TIME	BLOOD PRESSURE	PULSE	NOTES

DATE TIME	BLOOD PRESSURE	PULSE	NOTES

DATE TIME	BLOOD PRESSURE	PULSE	NOTES

DATE TIME	BLOOD PRESSURE	PULSE	NOTES

DATE TIME	BLOOD PRESSURE	PULSE	NOTES

DATE TIME	BLOOD PRESSURE	PULSE	NOTES

DATE TIME	BLOOD PRESSURE	PULSE	NOTES

DATE TIME	BLOOD PRESSURE	PULSE	NOTES

DATE TIME	BLOOD PRESSURE	PULSE	NOTES

DATE TIME	BLOOD PRESSURE	PULSE	NOTES

DATE TIME	BLOOD PRESSURE	PULSE	NOTES

DATE TIME	BLOOD PRESSURE	PULSE	NOTES

DATE TIME	BLOOD PRESSURE	PULSE	NOTES

DATE TIME	BLOOD PRESSURE	PULSE	NOTES

DATE TIME	BLOOD PRESSURE	PULSE	NOTES

DATE TIME	BLOOD PRESSURE	PULSE	NOTES

DATE TIME	BLOOD PRESSURE	PULSE	NOTES

DATE TIME	BLOOD PRESSURE	PULSE	NOTES

DATE TIME	BLOOD PRESSURE	PULSE	NOTES

DATE TIME	BLOOD PRESSURE	PULSE	NOTES

DATE TIME	BLOOD PRESSURE	PULSE	NOTES

DATE TIME	BLOOD PRESSURE	PULSE	NOTES

DATE TIME	BLOOD PRESSURE	PULSE	NOTES

DATE TIME	BLOOD PRESSURE	PULSE	NOTES

DATE TIME	BLOOD PRESSURE	PULSE	NOTES

DATE TIME	BLOOD PRESSURE	PULSE	NOTES

DATE TIME	BLOOD PRESSURE	PULSE	NOTES

DATE TIME	BLOOD PRESSURE	PULSE	NOTES

DATE TIME	BLOOD PRESSURE	PULSE	NOTES

DATE TIME	BLOOD PRESSURE	PULSE	NOTES

DATE TIME	BLOOD PRESSURE	PULSE	NOTES

DATE TIME	BLOOD PRESSURE	PULSE	NOTES

DATE TIME	BLOOD PRESSURE	PULSE	NOTES

DATE TIME	BLOOD PRESSURE	PULSE	NOTES

DATE TIME	BLOOD PRESSURE	PULSE	NOTES

DATE TIME	BLOOD PRESSURE	PULSE	NOTES

DATE TIME	BLOOD PRESSURE	PULSE	NOTES

DATE TIME	BLOOD PRESSURE	PULSE	NOTES

DATE TIME	BLOOD PRESSURE	PULSE	NOTES

DATE TIME	BLOOD PRESSURE	PULSE	NOTES

DATE TIME	BLOOD PRESSURE	PULSE	NOTES

DATE TIME	BLOOD PRESSURE	PULSE	NOTES

DATE TIME	BLOOD PRESSURE	PULSE	NOTES

DATE TIME	BLOOD PRESSURE	PULSE	NOTES

DATE TIME	BLOOD PRESSURE	PULSE	NOTES

DATE TIME	BLOOD PRESSURE	PULSE	NOTES

DATE TIME	BLOOD PRESSURE	PULSE	NOTES

DATE TIME	BLOOD PRESSURE	PULSE	NOTES

DATE TIME	BLOOD PRESSURE	PULSE	NOTES

DATE TIME	BLOOD PRESSURE	PULSE	NOTES

DATE TIME	BLOOD PRESSURE	PULSE	NOTES

DATE TIME	BLOOD PRESSURE	PULSE	NOTES

DATE TIME	BLOOD PRESSURE	PULSE	NOTES

DATE TIME	BLOOD PRESSURE	PULSE	NOTES

DATE TIME	BLOOD PRESSURE	PULSE	NOTES

DATE TIME	BLOOD PRESSURE	PULSE	NOTES

DATE TIME	BLOOD PRESSURE	PULSE	NOTES

DATE TIME	BLOOD PRESSURE	PULSE	NOTES

DATE TIME	BLOOD PRESSURE	PULSE	NOTES

DATE TIME	BLOOD PRESSURE	PULSE	NOTES

DATE TIME	BLOOD PRESSURE	PULSE	NOTES

DATE TIME	BLOOD PRESSURE	PULSE	NOTES

DATE TIME	BLOOD PRESSURE	PULSE	NOTES

DATE TIME	BLOOD PRESSURE	PULSE	NOTES

DATE TIME	BLOOD PRESSURE	PULSE	NOTES

DATE TIME	BLOOD PRESSURE	PULSE	NOTES

DATE TIME	BLOOD PRESSURE	PULSE	NOTES

DATE TIME	BLOOD PRESSURE	PULSE	NOTES

DATE TIME	BLOOD PRESSURE	PULSE	NOTES

DATE TIME	BLOOD PRESSURE	PULSE	NOTES

DATE TIME	BLOOD PRESSURE	PULSE	NOTES

DATE TIME	BLOOD PRESSURE	PULSE	NOTES

DATE TIME	BLOOD PRESSURE	PULSE	NOTES

DATE TIME	BLOOD PRESSURE	PULSE	NOTES